The Prospects for Zero Inflation

- Imon Ghosh

The Prospects for Zero Inflation

Dedication

For my wife Tanusree
and for our daughter Nayantara
who was a gleam in our eye
(in 1984) even though
her name was already
chosen.

Table of Contents

Title Page

Copyright Page

Dedication

Table of Contents

Foreword by Ambassador K.P. Fabian

The Imon's Imprints Public Policy Advocacy Series

Preface

Chapter 1:   Inflation is unpleasant

Chapter 2:   What causes the money supply to grow?

Chapter 3:   A printing press phenomenon

Chapter 4:   Binges and hangovers

Chapter 5:   No full employment

without inflation?

Chapter 6:   A rising tide of inflation

Chapter 7:   Would a gold standard help?

Chapter 8:   "A consumption yet incurable."

Chapter 9:   Making democracy even more democratic

Chapter 10:   Some concluding thoughts

End Notes

About the Author

Foreword

By Ambassador K.P. Fabian

In 1984 Imon Ghosh handed me a copy of his book *The Prospects for Zero Inflation.* I was struck by the brevity and the elegant but rigorous reasoning of the book on a subject of vital importance. I am glad that the book is being republished as its value and relevance to our times are in no way diminished by the passage of time.

I recall a conversation in 1991 with Dr. Manmohan Singh, the Finance Minister who opened up India's economy. We were on a flight to Bombay from Delhi. I asked him: While tackling inflation, apart from looking at the statistics given by his officials, did he consult one or two house wives? He asked a counter question: Why should the house wives be consulted as the officials gave scientifically accurate figures. I responded that the decision makers should know how inflation affected and afflicted the household. I do not think I won the argument. I honestly feel that Imon's book should be read by our policy makers, bureaucratic and political.

Imon is a polymath, a dwindling tribe as nowadays scholars know more and more about the less and less. An over mathematicized Economics is divorced from the ground realities. We need to bring back the Political Economy of the 19th century and move away from the Economic Sciences of the 20th century. Imon has made a singular contribution by showing us that it is possible to have a people-centred economics. His ideas about taxation in chapter 9 deserve attention. Imon has wisely argued the case for the tax payers to have a major say in how the money they paid is spent. We the public will be glad to see another book from the same author focused on this matter with actionable recommendations appropriate to the largest democracy.

This book should be translated into other languages, Indian and foreign, as it is of universal interest.

K.P. Fabian

Professor, Indian Institute of International Law
Former Ambassador of India
to Finland, Qatar, and Italy.

New Delhi

7th May, 2017

About the Imon's Imprints Public Policy Advocacy Series, and The Inclusive Growth & Financial Stability Forum

The Imon's Imprints Advocacy Series seeks to enhance lives by informing public policy, with the aim of improving it.

Besides sensitizing the public about key issues, and policy makers about policy alternatives involving inflation and monetary and fiscal policy under the aegis of the Inclusive Growth and Financial Stability Forum, the Public Policy Advocacy Series will explore other issues of interest as well.

About the Inclusive Growth and Financial Stability Forum:

As economic growth around the world slows down, and income inequality widens in many countries, it is imperative to identify and nurture new engines of economic growth that are both inclusive and sustainable.

I created the Inclusive Growth and Financial Stability Forum to enable its members to explore ideas, and advocate policies, that promote inclusive economic growth and, in particular, explore its linkages to global financial stability. This volume contributes to that debate.

Another major publication of the Inclusive Growth and Financial Stability Forum addresses accelerating economic growth by reducing poverty.

Preface

This book was first published in September 1984 in a soft as well as hard bound edition. It was self-published, and I went to considerable efforts doing so (besides the writing, which was a pleasure because I was already becoming passionate about a subject I had disliked in high school!) as a twentieth birthday gift to myself.

Typewriters were in widespread use then. Although the first personal computers had been introduced a decade earlier in the form of kits, and IBM had launched its personal computer in 1981, they were few and far between in 1984. Dot matrix printers predominated. Although the Advertising Agency I worked at as a Copywriter used phototypesetting for the press ads that we produced (mostly cut and pasted by the Art Department), it was not cost-effective to typeset my entire book. So I typed it instead on A4 sheets of paper, and took photocopies of each page at around 65% of its original size to get an approximation of a typeset page.

I recall wishing at the time that computers became more affordable, and had programs that allowed type fonts to be set, and books written in sophisticated fonts similar to the *What You See Is What You Get* (WYSIWYG) that the expensive phototypesetting permitted, at comparable quality standards. This wish, and technology, has come to pass and has been available for many years now…

Although publishing a soft cover edition of the book was easy, the hard cover edition posed several challenges since I wanted to use artificial leather. Book binders told me it could not be done. However, after some research and development followed by plenty of trial and error, I eventually produced elegant hard bound copies with gold foil lettering of the title on the cover.

One such hard bound copy (minus the gold foil lettering on the cover, which had worn off over the years) that I had gifted to my late father has survived in good condition, and came into my possession after he passed away. It is from this copy that I have reconstructed this edition, verbatim. Other than dividing my original monograph into ten chapters, I have retained the original version unchanged even though some of the ideas make me wince … and many more make me proud of my 19-year-old self.

The 1984 edition of this book was a labour of love. Copies were displayed at several bookstores in Cochin, Kerala (where I was also a regular customer, and had a relationship with the book store owners or managers), and one was sold to the Chairman of my Advertising Agency, the late Mr. John Chakola. All the other copies were given away to friends, or gifted to libraries. Not exactly what you might call a commercial success!

This Kindle, CreateSpace, and audiobook edition remains a labour of love. I am told that publishing paradigms have changed since 1984, and while I shall be curious to see whether Amazon's digital platform and global marketplace will impact this edition's commercial success, I shall be pleased if the book influences public policy resulting in lower rates of inflation and greater financial stability.

Imon Ghosh

Kolkata, India

7th May, 2017

Chapter 1

Inflation is unpleasant

Inflation is unpleasant, and usually leads to unfortunate social consequences. Larger sections of the population find their noses beneath water. The decrease in purchasing power undermines the ability of companies to sell the goods they produce. This leads to stagflation. Capital formation is adversely affected, and so is productive output. The nation's currency is depreciated on foreign exchange markets. Carried far enough, inflation can pave the way for social disorder and economic chaos (as the German inflation did in the 1920s).

Inflation is defined as an increase in aggregate price levels, and is measured by a price index (usually the Consumer Price Index or, less frequently, by the GNP deflator).

"A study of economics reveals that the best time to buy anything is last year."

\- Marty Allen

Prices of individual commodities, seldom stationary, tend to bounce about the place, reflecting the supply and demand situation. An increase (even a sharp one) in the price of a given commodity, therefore, does not constitute inflation.

Increases in aggregate price levels are evident with a decline in the purchasing power of money - an erosion of its store of value - indicating an imbalance in the control of the money supply.

The manner in which we control our money supply reminds me of the 'Vector Theory of Systems', which states that systems run better when designed to run downhill!

No nation likes to have a tissue paper currency. I certainly wouldn't like to see the rupee become one. What, then, is to be done about inflation?

A short-term solution for inflation that is popular with governments the world over (especially during an election year) is wage and price controls.[1] Ineffective at best, price and wage controls can have, when ineptly administered, an adverse effect on productive output.

Shultz's Law

Price controls work best when they are needed least.

Price controls can, to use a close analogy, be likened to holding a beach ball beneath the surface of a pool of water. There is a strong tendency for the ball - as there are for the prices - to rise to a state of equilibrium (in this analogy, the surface of the pool).

The opposite also happens to be true. It would be possible to hold our ball above the surface of the water, but it will only remain there as long as the hand that is holding it up (government regulated price floors) doesn't let go, when the ball, unable to support itself, will return rapidly to equilibrium…

Obviously, we are going to find it increasingly difficult to hold down aggregate price levels if we continue to inflate the money supply (… raise the level of water in our metaphorical swimming pool).

The way to bring our prices down, without having to 'push them below surface' with price controls and striving to keep them there, would be to drain some water gently from our swimming pool (or at least refrain from filling it up so fast!). And presto! Before our very eyes we see those inflated prices floating down within our reach … and hopefully, we find we can soon breathe again!

Like many things in life, what is called for here is moderation. The first duty of the government is to keep the economy liquid (the equivalent of ensuring that there is sufficient water in the swimming pool, and circulating it to prevent it from stagnating). John Maynard Keynes employed his genius suggesting ways the government could do just that, after the 'pool had run dry' during the depression years.

The scenario today is very different. Our pool floweth over, leaving those who can't swim (hedge against inflation) in the deep end.

"That money talks
I'll not deny,
I heard it once:
It said, "Goodbye".
- Richard Armour

Chapter 2

What causes the money supply to grow?

What, in this age of inflation, determines the growth of the money supply?

The government alone (and rightly so) is empowered to create money - either by a stroke of the bookkeeper's magic pen, or by printing the stuff.

"When government talks about 'raising capital' it means printing it."
- Peter F. Drucker

The government appears to shadow what is loosely called 'the demand for money' -

that is, the willingness to save it, as a measure of the confidence in its store of value.

Shadowing the 'demand for money' to determine the growth of the money supply is about as impractical an activity for the government to engage in as chasing butterflies in summer. It is the cause of much of the inflation we experience, and hardly represents the moderation that is urgently called for.

The moderation I recommend involves refraining from expanding the money supply in excess or - I must add - short of, the growth in the output of goods and services (with a small margin on either side, if required, for breathing space). This strategy is designed to prevent too much money from chasing too few goods.

A measure of this nature, however, isn't likely to be popular with the government, which has a vested interest in inflating the money supply by as much as it can get away with. The government is the first user of all the money it creates. Inflation allows it to repay its debts with cheaper rupees, as well as benefit from bracket creep.

"If the government doesn't believe in (the importance of) the currency (retaining its value), who will."
- George W.J. Goodman

I don't mean to sound harsh. That doesn't escape the fact that the social consequences of an inflationary policy are terrible. Heed, if you will, the words of Lord Keynes:

"There is no subtler, no surer means of overturning the existing basis of society than to debauch the currency."

"A disordered currency is one of the greatest political evils."
- Daniel Webster

What about the massive unemployment, and the likelihood of a recession, that will result if this strategy is carried through?

James Callaghan, former British prime minister, answered this question in 1976 when he said, "We used to think that you could just spend your way out of a recession and increase employment by cutting taxes and boosting government spending (by printing new currency). I tell you, in all candour, that this option no longer exists;

and insofar as it ever did, it only worked by injecting bigger doses of inflation into the economy followed by higher levels of unemployment at the next step. That is the history of the past twenty years."[2]

The policy of expanding the money supply in excess of the growth in productive output is, as we have seen, iatrogenic: It is a disease introduced by the doctor; one that may kill the patient, instead of curing him … And yet, most governments today continue to do so.

The advantage of expanding the money supply within the limits of productive output is that one avoids the problems associated with inflation and deflation (both dirty words), replacing them with what economists like to call 'disinflation' and 'reflation'.

Fine. What about demand-pull inflation? That has little to do with the money supply.

Demand-pull inflation isn't really inflation in the strictest sense, but only a reflection of the relative scarcity of a product.

Demand-pull inflation becomes a problem when supply isn't allowed to mobilize to meet demand. It affects (one hopes) relatively few products, and isn't greatly influenced by the money supply (except when people begin to lose faith in their currency). Breeding grounds for demand-pull inflation include: Government intervention in the economy; the stagnation of productivity (the two, unfortunately, aren't mutually exclusive); protectionism;

the inability to develop inexpensive substitutes for scarce or non-renewable resources, etc.

The term 'demand-pull inflation' is, in my opinion, a misnomer: Demand isn't the culprit for the inflation, if you can call it that. Supply is.

Cost-push inflation, on the other hand, reflects a general increase in prices across the board (a rise in the level of water, to use our marine metaphor once again, as opposed to the crests and troughs of individual waves associated with demand-pull inflation), a reliable indication that the growth in the quantity of money has exceeded an increase in output of goods and services.

Chapter 3

A printing press phenomenon

Inflation in our times, observes Professor Milton Friedman, is a printing press phenomenon.[3]

That's perhaps why we are bewildered when the prices don't respond, as they should, to good harvests and bountiful rains. We talk of 'speculative pressures' as if they really mattered. We ignore the fact that government presses keep churning out rupees by the thousands of crores, seemingly out of thin air.[4]

One prays that this will in some way benefit

the poor, because they are the hardest hit by inflation.

The question needs to be asked: Why do governments risk social turmoil to raise the extra money?

"There does not seem to be a unified constituency for preserving the integrity of money."

- George W.J. Goodman

At first sight the government appears to benefit by undermining the economy (it does this whenever it receives utility without creating any).

The benefit, however, is illusory ... because you cannot win while everybody else loses. (This goes against the grain of Lester

Thurow's Zero-Sum Society, where the winners gain at the expense of the losers.[5])

"The money is the same, only
the pockets are different."
- Gertrude Stein

Any gains from inflation are temporary. We all lose to inflation in the medium run …

"A phenomenon noticeable throughout
history regardless of place or period is the
pursuit by governments of policies contrary
to their own interests."
- Barbara W. Tuchman

There is ample evidence in history to show that inflation can undermine governments that print their way into it.

The collapse of the Weimar Republic under the weight of a worthless currency ought to serve as a reminder and a warning: It led to the rise of Nazism.

"The road to dictatorship will be open to any man who can persuasively promise security to all."
- Will and Ariel Durant

Hyperinflation after the First World War in Russia, where prices sometimes doubled from one day to the next, resulted from the fact that the Tsar found it convenient to finance his expenses, as well as the war, by printing additional currency.

A similar inflation in China under Chiang Kai-shek after the Second World War ended in similar results.

The solution most often put forward for inflation is increased productivity. This certainly helps (as long as the expansion of the money supply is kept under rein).

Brazil, which achieved one of the highest rates of growth in output, was productive enough. The expansion of its money supply, however, outpaced its gains in productivity … and today Brazil has one of the highest rates of inflation found anywhere - along with a host of social problems, including tragic food riots.

If the rate of inflation is pushed high enough in my country, I predict a military take-over (ostensibly to restore law and order and 'make the trains run on time' … even though our Amnesty record is unlikely to improve), preceded by extreme social strife of the sort that India experiences in her unhappier moments - something I wouldn't like to see happen.

Is zero inflation possible? I believe it is. (Arthur Burns, former head of the U.S. Federal Reserve System, apparently thought so too. When asked what he considered an acceptable rate of inflation, he replied, "An acceptable rate of inflation? An acceptable rate? Why, zero. Zero!"[6])

While I subscribe to the view that there are no simple solutions to inflation (please keep your solutions as complicated as possible!), I have developed a metaphor that attempts to simplify the issues involved:

The wage-price spiral, assumed to 'feed on one another', is replaced by the imagery of

a beach ball floating on a pool of water –
rising as the level of water rises (cost-push
inflation), and bobbing up and down on the
crests and troughs of individual waves
(demand-pull inflation).

As an afterthought, perhaps a jacuzzi (with
its outlets plugged) would better describe
the flow of high-powered money into the
economy!

Chapter 4

Binges and hangovers

Economists have known for a number of years that a rapid increase in the money supply will lead to inflation.

Milton Friedman, noted monetary economist and Nobel prize winner, estimates that an excessive growth in the money supply takes about six months to find its way through a healthy economy before being transformed into aggregate price increases.[7] Sooner for an economy less healthy.

This brief period between monetary expansion and inflation is characterised by general economic euphoria, greater output, higher employment – and, needless to say, greater government spending. *Then, the 'morning after', comes the hangover.* In economic terms this means lower output, higher unemployment and greater inflation.

The government at this point can do one of two things: The hangover isn't a permanent state of affairs (they seldom are), and can be allowed to run its course. Or, the government can ease the hangover by inflating the money supply yet again.

"Affairs of state are operated so that one generation pays for the debts of the last generation by issuing bonds to the next generation."

- Laurence J. Peter

Once the economy is hooked into this self-destructive pattern, it takes progressively larger 'fixes' of high-powered money to 'kick' the economy into the same 'high'. The effects of inflation can be as harmful to the economy as drug abuse can to the individual. (Not something a self-respecting government would indulge in.)

It is fashionable today to criticise the "monetarist's viewpoint" (essentially, what I have stated above) as naïve and simplistic. Inflation is thought to be mysterious and undecipherable – and, as such, not to be given much thought.

"Where it is a duty to worship the sun, it is pretty sure to be a crime to examine the laws of heat."

- John Morely

Friedman himself has drawn a considerable amount of flak from a number of economists who hold the view that an expansion of the money supply isn't largely responsible for inflation (just as some U.S. government officials continue to insist that there is no relationship whatsoever between government deficits and increases in interest rates), perhaps because they have a stake in government spending.

Truman's Law

If you can't convince them, confuse them.

A lot of talent is required to be taken for a waltz with these arguments. The relationship between government deficits and interest rates, for example, is direct and uncomplicated:

A deficit occurs whenever a government spends more than it taxes. Governments can finance deficits in two ways, both of which will raise the rates of interest. (A) It can borrow the money (and with its 'no-risk' credit rating, invariably gets the lion's share), leaving other borrowers to scramble for what's left, and driving up the interest rates in the process.[8] Or, (B) it can print the money, prompting tighter monetary controls – which means larger reserve requirements and higher interest rates…

The significance of a rise in interest rates is that it discourages investment.

In countries where there are no good bond markets, governments find it difficult to borrow from the private sector. Therefore, they tend to finance their deficits directly by printing money.[2]

Another myth relating to the expansion of the money supply that deserves a close look is that of deposit expansion.

Students of economics are told with a straight face (possibly because their professors believe it themselves) that bank deposits, when lent out, expand the money supply. The suggestion is that, somehow, more money is created in the process than was there before. (The deposit banks are then credited with having manufactured the money…)

This interesting proposition, however, only looks at one half of the equation: If money appears to have been 'magically' created, it is to those who have borrowed it, for they now have access to credit they didn't have before. The other half of the equation, of course, is that the depositors who put up the money abstained from using it, even if temporarily.

The argument runs that since depositors and borrowers have checking accounts and drawing rights to the sums due them, overall credit is expanded.

A situation where everyone drew most of their money simultaneously from the bank, and additional credit was created (Aha!) can only last a brief while (an analogy here is virtual matter in particle physics), usually before all the cheques are processed, and the bank files for insolvency ...

(With electronic fund transfers, even this brief 'float' disappears.)

The system works because depositors and borrowers, with drawing rights to the same pool of money, can't (or if they can, don't choose to) exercise that right simultaneously.

In time deposits, out of which most loans are made, depositors forfeit the use of their money for a specified period of time.

Viewed from this perspective, deposit expansion is as substantial as the emperor's new clothes.

(If I appear to have stated the obvious, you are invited to open an economics textbook of your choice to 'deposit expansion' under 'money and banking' for a treatise to the contrary.)

What does happen when depositors put their money in banks (esp. into time deposits) is that some central bankers says (probably to himself), "Well now, we have more money in the savings pool that can absorb an expansion of the money supply…"

It takes high-powered money to generate high-powered inflation.

Chapter 5

No full employment
without inflation?

Let us consider another piece of conventional wisdom: You Cannot Have Full Employment Without Inflation. (No-win situations like this one – I can't say I like them very much – contribute to the image of economics as a dismal science.)

"The Congress declares that it is the continuing responsibility of the federal government to ... promote maximum employment, production, and purchasing power."

- U.S. Employment Act, 1946

The trade-off between inflation and unemployment is expressed mathematically by the Phillips Curve. Named after the English economist, A.W. Phillips who formulated it in the 1950s, the Phillips Curve showed a generation of policymakers the way to reduce unemployment.

(The trade-off, I believe, was meant to be between unemployment and aggregate supply, and not inflation and unemployment...)

It was subsequently discovered that you could have a higher rate of inflation and increased unemployment (like having your cake and eating it); that it is easier to reduce unemployment (for a while) by inflating the money supply, than it is to reduce inflation by fostering unemployment; that the

Phillips Curve resembles a spiral…

Where did the Phillips Curve go wrong? It assumed that the government alone is capable of creating full employment, by "stimulating the economy" (into inflationary growth). Professor Phillips, however, deserves no discredit. He had foresight … while we have the advantage of hindsight (a perfect '20/20').

"Small businesses, not big corporations, are responsible for most of the new jobs created and most of the nation's economic growth."
                                    - John Naisbitt

The venture capital pool in the United States virtually dried up in 1969 when the capital-gains tax was raised from 25 to 49%. In 1968, 300 new high-tech companies were founded in the U.S., while not one came into existence in 1976 (...the government was busy 'stimulating the economy' throughout this period in an effort to increase employment). In 1978, the capital-gains tax was reduced from 49 to 28%. Accordingly, venture capital shot up from $39m in 1977 to $570m in 1978. The capital-gains tax is now down to 20% under the Reagan administration.[10]

The venture capital pool, an important tool for creating additional employment, pales into insignificance besides government deficits. (The U.S. government isn't above an occasional attempt to make the invisible hand disappear...)

And then there's the "Full Employment Rate of Unemployment": A teenager looking for his first job, regardless of how much he may need it, isn't counted among the unemployed, since he hasn't yet entered the labour force.

(You'd have to be employed, to be unemployed.) Having been a teenager looking for a job myself, I appreciate how narrow this definition can seem.

Peter's Financial Law

Starting from scratch is easy;
It's starting without it that's tough.

Once you are in the labour force, however, you can count on the privilege of being labelled "Unemployed" every time you are out of a job.

"Unemployment has become such an intrinsic feature of our economy that government economists now speak of "full employment" when more than five percent of the labour force is out of work."

- Fritjof Capra

Chapter 6

A rising tide of inflation

A progressive lowering of standards appears to characterise much of the activity of government, along with a talent for working at cross-purposes with its own objectives. This wouldn't interest us here if inflation wasn't linked intimately with government spending.

Schrank's Laws for Successful Administration

1. If a program doesn't work, expand it.

2. The bigger it gets, the less notice anyone will take when it isn't working.

Le Chatelier's Principle

Complex systems tend to oppose their own proper function.

The last and most decadent stage of any development is giantism. When one cannot think of how to do things better one simply makes things bigger. The construction of the great pyramids in Egypt marked the end of the Old Kingdom. Bigger and bigger cathedrals and temples were built when the faithful became secure and comfortable. Dinosaurs, too, were an evolutionary dead end.[11]

The trend today is towards rising inflation as the world rolls closer to greater statism, government spending, involvement and intervention in the economy.

"There has been an increase in the amount of government control. Much of this regulation can hardly be dignified by the title of 'planning'.
- Paul A. Samuelson

The Indian government hasn't fulfilled a single five year plan (targets it periodically sets for itself) since independence.

The fact that we've had intelligent and dedicated individuals heading, and staffing our government doesn't appear to have made much difference. India's social development continues to be presided over by a philosophy that's long on planning, and short on implementation.

The Indian economy has been described as having a long, and undisturbed siesta. I believe I'm familiar with the nature of the tranquilizer she takes with monotonous regularity. It keeps India from coming awake to her full potential...

I call the malady centralysis, and have formulated a law that describes its effects on the economy.

Imon's Currency Law

The harder the government, the

softer the currency.

People, of course, are far more important than the way some curve or index looks to an economist. Inflation, however, hurts everyone – including those who have a strong vested interest in the expansion of the money supply – and hinders the development of the economy.

Even the head of a socialist state has said that:

"If there is agreement about anything, it is in regard to inflation and corruption. Both are increasing, and both are eating into the vitals of our society."
- Smt. Indira Gandhi

A discounted cash flow analysis reveals that the present value of a rupee ten years from now, given an annual rate of inflation of 3%, will be 74 paisa. 7% inflation will reduce the value of the rupee to 51 paisa. 15% to 25 paisa. 25% to 11 paisa. 50% to 1.73 paisa.

Figures like these are responsible for the reminiscences about prices "in the good old days".

"One of the benefits of inflation is that kids can no longer get sick on a nickel's worth of candy."

- Journeyman Barber Magazine

(It now takes several dollars.)

In 1970, fifty seven countries had rates of inflation ranging from zero to five percent. By 1979, this number was down to twelve. On the other hand, no nation in 1970 had a rate of inflation of fifty percent or above. In 1979, there were eight countries in this category.[12]

The International Monetary Fund's recently released annual report for 1984 states that the weighted average rate of inflation in the Western hemisphere rose sharply from 78% in 1982 to 123% in 1983! These figures would be hard to beat (indeed, it would be dangerous to do so) and the Eastern hemisphere fared better in comparison...

A change in policy regarding inflation will occur only when there is a confluence of changing values and economic necessity, and not before.[13] The change will inevitably have to include a commitment to the non-proliferation of the nation's currency. Coming down to the finer points of control, however, we discover that ...

"Electorates are prone to replace any central banker or head of state who practices the simple nineteenth century virtues of fixed money supply with balanced budgets."

- Paul A. Samuelson

Chapter 7

Would a gold standard help?

It has been suggested that switching to a gold standard would help to stem inflation, and restore confidence in the currency. While this would serve to restrict an expansion of the money supply, gold isn't sensitive to the credit requirements of a dynamic economy.

I think it would be wiser to stick to token paper money, and then regulate it intelligently. This would enable the government to (literally) make some money on the sideline. And there's always the possibility that it will be put to good use…

"The golden age only comes to men when they have forgotten gold."
- G.K. Chesterton

Selective reflation, if handled with intelligence and imagination, could have a synergistic effect on productive output.

Lal's Law
Things are always getting better and worse in India at the same time.

"In 1958, every rupee invested in government enterprises yielded an average of 13 paisa; in 1965, it was 8 paisa. For private industry, the corresponding figures were 26 paisa and 35 paisa."
- Jay Dubashi

Many of the functions the Indian government monopolizes are vital to society. Inefficiency in these key areas can compromise the entire economy, as well as our social development.

The government of India appears to have abdicated its role as protector and benefactor of the poor. Instead, it has found ingenious ways of taxing them in their poverty, playing to their hopes and dreams by creating illusions of wealth (all of it taxable). Lotteries are big business in India, run primarily by the state governments to augment their revenues in violation of their injunctions against gambling.

You can't help being shocked and saddened at the ethics of a government that hawks its worthless confetti to the poor who can ill afford to part with the few rupees that they own. (The 'Robin Hood Complex', with its delusions of virtue, however, remain.)

"Corrupt, stupid, grasping functionaries will make at least as big a muddle of socialism as stupid, selfish and acquisitive employers can make of capitalism."
- Walter Lippmann

"Under capitalism, man exploits man. Under communism, the reverse is true."
- Polish Proverb

The Swedish donors of an aid package to India designated for the needy discovered to their chagrin that the aid, channelled through the government, was unable to filter through to the ranks of the poor.

"Nobody really believes anymore
that government delivers."

\- Peter F. Drucker

Chapter 8

"A consumption yet incurable."

A closer look at the structure of government financing, and the quality of its output would be in order, to get a firm grip on the problem of inflation.

"Each period of emergency, each war, each depression expands the activity of government. After such periods are over, government expenditure never seems to go back to previous levels."

\- Paul A. Samuelson

"The state is inclining to a consumption

yet incurable."

- Sir Edward Coke

A nation as poor as ours cannot afford many sinecures. Much of the government's expenses goes to support an insatiable bureaucracy that thrives on inputs, without undue consideration about outputs.

The problem of making government accountable is an old one, and yet it hasn't lost its currency...

"Bureaucracy defends the status quo long

past the time when the quo has lost its

status."

- Laurence J. Peter

The business of bureaucracy, from all

appearances, is to keep the bureaucracy in business… (I've always found it difficult to make a distinction between bureaucracy and government.)

"A bureaucrat rules by controlling the flow of information. If some application has to pass through his desk he can hold it up, send it back for resubmission or lose it – thus exercising complete power over anything that is channelled through him."
- Edward deBono

The person who is cast into the role of a bureaucrat deserves our sympathy, for he has to work with others who are too!

"We can lick gravity, but sometimes the paperwork is overwhelming."
- Wernher Von Braun

The economy pays dearly for a bureaucracy that is more concerned with activity, than it is with output.

"... Finally, there is the meeting which is called not because there is business to be done, but because it is necessary to create the impression that business is being done."
- John Kenneth Galbraith

Taxes, an economic disincentive with adverse effects on productive output, go hand in hand with the misutilization and wastage of resources within the bureaucracy.

"A process of development that wastes resources in the name of 'social cost' (it should do precisely the opposite, for real

development creates resources instead of
wasting them) is antisocial and doomed
from the start."

- Jay Dubashi

In the grim words of Arthur H. Robinson, "Civilization is doomed unless some way can be found to check the growth of bureaucracy."

India has one of the highest effective rates of taxation in the world, and one of its narrowest revenue bases. I suspect one has something to do with the other...

"Why does a slight tax increase cost you two hundred dollars and a substantial tax cut save you thirty cents?"

- Peg Bracken

"Taxes are going up so fast that the government is likely to price itself right out of the market."

\- Dan Bennett

"I have been reduced to penury by heavy taxation."

\- George Bernard Shaw

The social statist accuses the unwilling rich of equating taxes with death, and then proceeds to arrange their funeral...

"The primary requisite for any new tax law is for it to exempt enough voters to win the next elections."

\- Laurence J. Peter

There are many who will disagree with the opinions I've expressed here (...as well as many who won't). In all fairness, one has to grant that economists who don't share your point of view also have the best interests of society in mind.

"If all economists were laid end to end, they would not reach a conclusion."
- George Bernard Shaw

I occasionally find it useful to take myself with a grain of salt – not because I'm wrong … but because I don't wish to be inflexible, or dogmatic (for then one would have ceased to think).

"Many of today's economic problems are yesterday's solutions."
- Arnold Glasow

Bearing this in mind with the appropriate

humility, I shall proceed to propose a new form of taxation, one that can make democracy even more democratic...

Chapter 9

Making democracy even more democratic

Taxes in existence today resemble a protection money racket. Every single one contains within it an element of extortion.

This embarrassing fact is justified, and even made respectable, by what I've called the 'Robin Hood Complex'.

Whether any given tax constitutes a disincentive depends largely on the taxpayer's perception of how well his money is put to use.

Even when he contributes to a worthy

cause, the process of extortion ensures that the taxpayer is deprived of the satisfaction (and the credit) of having done so.

"The trouble with being a breadwinner nowadays is that the government is in it for such a big slice."

\- Mary McCoy

The picture on the other side of the tax coin isn't any prettier. Extortion robs the government of its incentive to perform, and economize (the money pours in, regardless of output...) and makes the bureaucracy less accountable.

Admits Francois Mitterrand, France's socialist president, "Too much tax chokes our economy, limits production and limits incentives."

In a participative system of raising funds for public use, taxes will be voluntary and will no longer constitute a disincentive.

So that's my first proposal: Remove the element of extortion from all taxes, and make them voluntary.

When people put their money voluntarily into government projects, their interest and support for those projects will increase as a consequence.

To ensure that resource allocation within the government reflects social utility and the taxpayers priorities, and not bureaucratic manoeuvring designed to acquire larger budgets, I propose that the taxpayer be given the right to allocate his money to specific   departments   or   areas   of governmental activity, and that this money be   non-transferable   (except   when   in surplus).[14]

This   will   make   each   department individually responsible to the taxpayer for its performance.

I also propose, in the interests of economy and to keep the bureaucracy on its toes, that the government be denied a monopoly in any area of economic activity, without excluding it from participating, if it has the taxpayers' support.

"Somebody will find a way to do it for a fraction of what it costs the government."

- Gregg Fawkes

We ought, like Jeremy Bentham (1748 – 1832), to subject our institutions and government bureaucracies to ruthless scrutiny in terms of their social utility.

The government will receive continuous feedback about the popularity of its projects … and will only be given the resources to carry out its popular ones.

"Optimum lege suave et facile illud faciet consuetudo."

- Pythegoras

(Choose from the best; custom will make it pleasant and easy…)

Although I have a preference for limited government, the form of taxation I've outlined here allows for large government. (That's what I like about it.)

"While the state exists, there is no freedom.
When there is freedom, there will be no
state."
- Nikolai Lenin

"If the average man had his way, there
would probably never have been a state."
- Will and Ariel Durant

… It also makes it possible for the "State to
wither away".

Ben Franklin, one of America's founding
fathers, described himself as "A Friend of
Vertue … a mortal Enemy to arbitrary
Government and unlimited Power."

Voluntary taxation won't be utopia, but it
will encourage society to take greater

initiative in solving its own problems.

It will give citizens the opportunity to determine the size, and direction of government's activities, and make democracy a little more democratic.

The economy, in turn, will receive a powerful boost with the removal of taxes and tariffs that limits its potential.

The nation's efforts would then be directed at strengthening the social fabric, and not the government...

"I know of no better depository of the ultimate powers of society than the people themselves."
- Thomas Jefferson

A question that continues to trouble me is whether a voluntary form of taxation will compromise the welfare of the elderly, the poor and others who require social assistance to survive.

I do not believe it is in the interests of any society to turn a Nelson's eye on its poor.

The economy, in my view, is organic – not mechanic. If any part of one's body is sick, or dying, the other parts are sure to be in trouble.

Even the rich, greedy, selfish capitalist loses valuable markets to poverty. Equally important, he (or she) loses the range of goods and services that would otherwise have been available if the poor weren't down and out.

A society that refuses to look after its needy cannot fail to sow the seeds of the grapes of wrath.

"The great companies did not know that the line between hunger and anger is a thin line."
- John Steinbech

"If a free society cannot help the many who are poor, it cannot save the few who are rich."
- John F. Kennedy

Chapter 10

Some concluding thoughts

"An empty stomach is not a good political advisor."

- Albert Einstein

The Indian government isn't equal to the task of sustaining the minimum standards of nutrition and health of every poor person in this country. It simply does not have the resources to do so. A major constraint is our large, and growing population. The government has a number of population control programmes, and appears to be doing a good job implementing them.

Unable to feed, clothe or look after the poor, the government has retreated to controlling the key infrastructural sectors of our economy. Judging from the performance of the state-run enterprises, and the unfulfilled 5 year plans, it hasn't done very well…

Society can either pay a bureaucracy to look after the welfare of the needy … or it can find more direct, and perhaps more effective ways of doing so: Ways that give the donor the satisfaction and credit for having done a good deed; that do not compromise the dignity of the recipient, or exchange security for religious indoctrination.

We would then see the emergence of a welfare society, in the place of a welfare state.

A humane society will not find it difficult to put into practice Marx's famous precept:

"From each according to his abilities; to each according to his needs."

(Article 14 of the Soviet Constitution of 1977 restates this as: "From each according to his abilities; to each according to his work.")

At some point we are going to have to look beyond the quantity, and look at the quality of our economic lives (those who wish to stay with the quantity are free to do so…).

You can't buy your way up Maslow's ladder. Money serves a useful, and necessary function on the lower rungs of Maslow's hierarchy, but it makes a poor substitute for meaningful relationships, self-actualization and self-esteem…

"To have or to be?"

- Erich Fromm

(That is the question.)

Voluntary taxation may be an answer to the age-old question of "Who will guard the guardians?" Society will. In a sense it always has…

I'll be elaborating on these ideas, and other issues relating to voluntary taxation, in another book.

Economics, like every other academic discipline, has its high priests to a hidden code. They feel uncomfortable in the presence of simplicity. Yet, as Khalil Gibran wrote many years ago, "The more complex the epoch, the simpler must be its solutions."

"Nothing is required, and nothing will avail, except a little, a very little, clear thinking."
- John Maynard Keynes

Every society, finally, gets the form of government it chooses, and deserves...

"A nation of sheep must in time beget a government of wolves."
- Bertrand de Jouvenel

"Followers create leaders. Period."
- John Naisbitt

Hitler, defining the virtues of dictatorship, once said that "The great strength of a totalitarian state is that it forces those who fear it to imitate it."

Prochnow's Law

The fellow who never makes a mistake takes his orders from someone who does.

If we want to see an end to inflation, and higher interest rates, the government must be discouraged from living beyond its means on deficit financing. (There will, under specified conditions, be Keynesian exceptions to this rule.) In formulating fiscal, and monetary policy, it is important to avoid being short-sighted.

A politician is credited with the insight that a week, in politics, is a very long time. Inflation, unfortunately, takes longer to cure.

The difference between a politician and a statesman, explains James Freeman Clarke, is that a politician thinks of the next elections and a statesman thinks of the next generation.

"We shall not pass on to our children less than our parents gave us."
- Lech Walesa

"Blessed are the young, for they shall inherit the national debt."
- Herbert Hoover

Indeed they shall ... unless the government is willing to exercise greater social responsibility, and fiscal restraint.

Like our blood pressure, the money supply and its velocity of circulation seldom attracts our attention, or elicits our concern, unless something goes terribly wrong...

The guardians of our currency owe it to the rest of us not to compromise long-term stability for short-term growth.

"The bane of India is the plethora of politicians and the paucity of statesmen."
- Nani Palkhivala
(We have one stateswoman.)

Zero inflation can be achieved, and maintained.

I believe the Indian government has the resolve and the intelligence to implement, in the best interests of this country, whatever strategy is necessary to reverse the trend that is taking us closer to a tissue paper currency.

Imon Ghosh

Cochin, India

September 26th, 1984

End Notes

1. See Imon's Laws of Price Control.

2. Quoted by MILTON and ROSE FRIEDMAN in 'Free to Choose' (Pelican, 1981) pp. 311-2

3. Ibid., p. 299.

4. Our Reserve Bank has succeeded in combining an excessive growth of the money supply with a coin shortage! This has created a unique kind of inflation, especially in the larger metropolitan centres like Bombay, with customers sometimes paying upto a rupee more than the list price on purchases. Storeowners

have began issuing coupons to tide over the shortage…

5. LESTER THUROW, 'The Zero-Sum Society' (Basic Books, New York, 1980) p. 42.

6. Adam Smith, 'Paper Money' (Futura, London, 1981) p. 16. This book is written under a nom de plume by GEORGE W.J. GOODMAN. I owe this masterful writer a special word of thanks for bringing to life a subject I used to hate.

7. FRIEDMAN, op. cit., p. 306.

8. The interest on public debt paid by the United States government during

the fiscal year 1980 along added up to $ 56,900,000,000 ... fifty six point nine billion dollars! Source: United States Office of Management and Budget.

9. STANLEY   FISCHER   and RUDIGER   DORNBUSCH, 'Economics', (McGraw Hill, 1983) p. 781.

10. JOHN   NAISBITT,   'Megatrends' (Warner Books, New York, 1984) p. 163.

11. HEINZ R. PAGELS, 'The Cosmic Code'   (ISBN   0-553-23128-6). Regrettably, I don't have the edition, or the page number available with me. This well written book surveys

the foundations, and the frontiers of quantum mechanics.

12. FISCHER and DORNBUSCH, op. cit., p. 755, table 31-1; IMF International Financial Statistics, various issues.

13. To paraphrase JOHN NAISBITT.

14. In the post-industrial information society that ALVIN TOFFLER, and JOHN NAISBITT have described so well, these surpluses can be avoided.

About the Author

Imon Ghosh is Founder of the Inclusive Growth and Financial Stability Forum, and is an NHRDN National Professor. He has a long standing interest in reducing poverty to accelerate economic growth.

Imon is a senior management professional with over 25 years of experience in the corporate sector and academia, including heading the Learning and Development function in India for a Fortune 100 MNC, teaching Economics at an International School, Management School and a Law University, and serving as Director of the Academy of HRD, India's premier institution specializing in human resources development for all organizational forms.

Imon is a Life Member of the All India Management Association, Indian Science Congress Association, Indian Society for Training & Development (ISTD) and the Indian Economic Association (among others) and has been an Individual Member of Gateway House: Indian Council on Global Relations.

Imon has served as a National Board Member of India's National HRD Network, and as Chairman of the Board of Studies for Management and Finance at the Nirma University Institute of Law. He is a Senior Consultant to the United Nations Institute for Training & Research (UNITAR) and has designed and taught a course on Training and Development at the Indian Institute of Management, Ranchi.

Imon has designed and delivered corporate training and faculty development programs with a special focus on Leadership Development to several thousand participants of many different nationalities in five countries and four continents for over two decades, with excellent participant feedback.

Besides inflation, Imon has written a book on *Reducing Poverty to Accelerate Economic Growth* in 1992. It has been republished under The Imon's Imprints Public Policy Advocacy Series, and is available on Amazon and elsewhere. In 2001, his book on *Reducing Poverty* was abridged and published on the Editorial page of *The Times of India*, and the article was later included in the records of the Indian Parliament. *Reducing Poverty to Accelerate Economic Growth* was also included in the syllabus of the National University of Juridical Sciences (NUJS) by its founding Vice Chancellor, Dr. Madhava Menon.

Imon contributed a chapter on *India's Sustainable Economic Growth, Challenges and Prospects* in the United Service Institution of India's Strategic Yearbook 2017 which was released by India's then Chief of Army Staff (and later India's first Chief of Defense Services), General Bipin Rawat, on 4th May 2017 in New Delhi. The United Service Institution of India (USI) is Asia's oldest think tank, established in 1870.

Readers are welcome to connect with Imon on Linkedin or email him at his personal email ID: imonghosh@gmail.com